M O

# MY FIRST PRAYERS

*A Book About
Talking to Jesus*

# CHARIOT
## FAMILY
# PUBLISHING
A DIVISION OF COOK COMMUNICATIONS

# This book belongs to

From

Chariot Books™ is an imprint of Chariot Family Publishing
Cook Communications, Colorado Springs, CO 80918
Cook Communications, Paris, Ontario
Kingsway Communications, Eastbourne, England

MY FIRST PRAYERS
©1995 by Cook Communications Ministries
All rights reserved. Except for brief excerpts for review purposes, no part of this
book may be reproduced or used in any form without written permission from the
publisher.
Cover illustration by Debby Anderson
First printing, 1995
Printed in Hong Kong
99 98 97 96 95            6 5 4 3 2
ISBN 0-7814-0210-7

# Contents

*Jesus said,*
*"Let the little children come to me,*
*and do not hinder them, for the king-*
*dom of God belongs to such as these.*
*I tell you the truth, anyone who will*
*not receive the kingdom of God like a*
*little child will never enter it."*
*Luke 18:16, 17 NIV*

# THANK YOU, JESUS

Dear Jesus,
Thank You for everything!

Thank You for songs to sing.

Thank You for
berries to pick.

Thank You, Jesus,
for spoons to lick.

Thank You for snow so cold.
Thank You for hands
to hold.

Thank You for the warm,
bright sun.
Thank You for room to run.

Thank You, Jesus,
for rocking chairs.
Thank You, Jesus,
for teddy bears.

Thank You for
a ladybug.

Thank You for
Grandpa's hug.

Thank You for
bunnies and puppies.
Thank You for
ducks and guppies.

Thank You, Jesus,
for quiet night.

Thank You
for morning light.

Thank You, Jesus,
for all I see.

Thank You for loving me.
In Jesus' name, Amen.

# THREE CHEERS
# FOR TODAY!

Good morning, Jesus!
It's a brand-new day.

I need to get up
and get going—
can't sleep it away!

Will it be sunny?
Will it be gray?

What will I do
with today?

Some days are for working;
I can help Mom or Dad.

Being a helper
will make me feel glad.

Some days are for playing,
for climbing a tree,

for splashing and dashing
and feeling free!

Some days are quiet, for
being still—

for thinking and praying
wherever I will.

Some days are happy,
some are sad,

but each is a special gift
from You, God.

This is the day the Lord has made; let us rejoice and be glad in it.

Psalm 118:24 NIV

So help me use it, not lose it.
It won't come by twice.

You made it, God, and it's
better than nice!
Thank You for today!
Amen.


*This is the day the Lord has made;
let us rejoice and
be glad in it.
Psalm 118:24 NIV*

*A friend loves at all times.*
*Proverbs 17:17a NIV*

# FRIENDS

Thank You, Jesus,
for friends.

Friends trust me, even with their brand-new crayons.

Friends are glad to see me.

Friends help me to try again.

Friends think
I am wonderful.

A friend is someone
I can pray for.

Jesus, You are my friend
forever and ever.

Friends love me anytime.

Friends forgive each other.

A friend can be
part of my family.

Friends help me look
for buried treasure.

Friends take care
of each other.

Friends know
when I need a hug.

Thank You, Jesus,
for friends to love.
In Jesus' name, Amen.

# TODAY IS
# FOR TRUSTING

Dear Jesus,
It's good to know I can
always count on You.

You show me
which way to go.

One of your promises says,
"Trust in the Lord with all
your heart . . . and he will
show you the right way."
Proverbs 3:5, 6 TEV

Jesus, You help me
to be brave.

Your Word, the Bible, tells me, "I trust in God and am not afraid; I praise him for what he has promised." Psalm 56:4 TEV

When everything is noisy and busy, I trust in You, God.

I know "You, Lord, give perfect peace to those who keep their purpose firm and put their trust in you."
Isaiah 26:3 TEV

When I feel weak or tired,
I trust You, Lord.

I remember the Bible verse that says, "Trust in the Lord God always, for in the Lord Jehovah is your everlasting strength."
Isaiah 26:4 TLB

God, You make life
really special!

The promise in Your Word
is true! "Put [your] hope
in God, who richly provides
us with everything for
our enjoyment."
I Timothy 6:17b NIV

I trust You, God, with my whole heart . . .

because You love me and are always watching out for me!

I trust in your unfailing
love; my heart rejoices
in your salvation.
Psalm 13:5 NIV
In Jesus Name, Amen.

*Children are a gift from the Lord.*
*Babies are a reward.*
*Psalm 127:3 ICB*

# BABIES ARE FOR LOVING

Thank You, Jesus, for babies.
They are one of Your
best ideas!

Babies are quiet when they're asleep.

Babies smile all over.

Babies like to
hold my hand.

Babies wonder
about things.

Babies eat peas
with their fingers.

Babies have a
lot to learn.

Babies smell so good—
when they are clean.

Babies are sometimes messy, soggy, and tired out.

Babies like to
do what I do.

Babies need me.

Babies like to help
in the kitchen.

Babies try hard.

I'm glad You love
babies, Jesus.
In Jesus' name, Amen.

*God, you have taught me
since I was young.
Psalm 71:17a ICB*

# HURRAY FOR BIRTHDAYS!

Hurray, God!
It's my birthday!

I can't lose a birthday or trade it; it's my very own.

It's free, but each year
I get only one.

Most people think it's
the best kind of fun.

It usually comes with good
things to eat . . .

sometimes with games and candles and treats . . .

always with special family
and friends. . . .

Yes—it's my birthday!
Let the party begin!

I like it, God, when
my family sings to me!

I have just one birthday;
it shows up each year.

# BIRTHDAY
# CERTIFICATE

Trent
_____
NAME

M
_____
BIRTH DATE

It's my day. I'm special
because You made me, God.
I'm one of a kind.
Before I was born,
You had me in mind.

*You saw me before I was born and
scheduled each day of my life before I
began to breathe. Every day was
recorded in your book!*
*Psalm 139:16 TLB*

You planned my birthday
before I was born,
so rat-a-tat, drum,
and tootle-toot, horn!

Hurray for birthdays!
In Jesus' name, Amen.

*Teach us to number our days aright,*
*that we may gain a heart of wisdom.*
*Psalm 90:12 NIV*

# ALL YEAR LONG

Thank You for the seasons
of the year, Jesus.

Summer tastes like strawberries, cherry tomatoes, and ice cream.

You love me
in the summer, God.

Autumn is a good time
to lie in the leaves.

Autumn smells like crayons, apples, and new school shoes.

You love me in
the autumn, God.

Winter is a good time
to help a neighbor.

Winter feels cold
on the outside and
warm on the inside.

Winter means making prints in fresh snow.

You love me in the winter, God.

Spring is a good time to
dance and play in
the warm grass.

Spring means sprouts.

Spring sounds like
quack-quack, cheep, baaa,
and happy giggles.

God, You love me in the
spring . . . and all year long.
In Jesus' name,
Amen.

*Love is patient, love is kind. It does
not envy, it does not boast,
it is not proud.
It is not rude, it is not self-seeking, it
is not easily angered, it keeps no
record of wrongs. Love does not
delight in evil but rejoices with the
truth. It always protects,
always trusts, always hopes,
always perseveres. . . .
And now these three remain:
faith, hope and love.
But the greatest of these is love.
I Corinthians 13:4-7, 13 NIV*

# LOVE IS
# KIND

If I don't have love, Jesus,
I am nothing.

Even if I were good and wise and generous, it wouldn't mean a thing without love.

Love is patient.
Love is kind.

Love isn't jealous.
Love doesn't brag.

Love isn't rude.
Love isn't selfish.

Love doesn't get mad easily.
Love doesn't keep
a list of wrongs.

Love is never happy about wrongdoing, but love is happy with truth.

Love always protects.
Love always trusts.

Love always hopes.
Love always keeps going.

Love never fails.

These three things
will last forever:
Faith,
Hope,
Love.

But the greatest of these . . .

is love.

Help me to love others as
You have loved me, God.
In Jesus' name,
Amen.

*Her children arise*
*and call her blessed.*
*Proverbs 31:28a NIV*

# MOMS ARE SPECIAL

Dear Jesus,
my mom is a special person.

She never gets tired.

She can make anything out of cardboard boxes.

She appreciates nature . . .
most of the time.

She doesn't always
let me win.

My mom has
quick reflexes.

She knows
what I'm up to.

She is there
when I need her.

She is understanding.
(Usually.)

My mom
believes in me.

She can be a little
bit embarrassing.

She cries at the
oddest times.

She never runs
out of hugs.

My mom is one of
Your best ideas, God!
Thank You for giving
her to me.
In Jesus' name, Amen.

*Love the Lord your God with all your heart and with all your soul and with all your strength. These commandments that I give you today are to be upon your hearts. Impress them on your children. Talk about them when you sit at home and when you walk along the road, when you lie down and when you get up.*
*Deuteronomy 6:5-7 NIV*

# HOME IS BEST

Dear Jesus,
thank You for my home
and the lessons I learn there.

Home is where I learn
right from wrong.

Home is where there's room
to make mistakes.

Home is listening to music.
Thank You for music, Jesus.

Home is where
we listen to each other.

Home is where we share
Your love, Jesus.

Home is where there's
room to be myself.

Home is the smell of buttered toast in the morning and clean sheets at night.

Home is where I don't have
to hurry . . . usually!

Home is feeling warm
when it's cold outside.

Home is the sound
of laughter and the taste of
popcorn. Thank You for fun
times with my family, Jesus.

Home is where
I am needed most.

Thank You, Jesus, that
home is where I belong.
In Jesus' name,
Amen.

*The angel said to the women, "Don't be afraid. I know that you are looking for Jesus, the one who was killed on the cross. But he is not here. He has risen from death as he said he would." Matthew 28:5, 6a ICB*

# EASTER IS HERE!

Dear Jesus, Easter is the most important day of the year.

That's because Easter
is You, Jesus, alive!

Easter is new life.

Easter is Your power
showing, God.

Easter is You at work
in me, Jesus.

Easter is a new song
in my heart.

I am SO GLAD You are alive,
Jesus! Thank You for
this wonderful day.
In Jesus' name,
Amen.

*Today in the town of David a Savior
has been born to you; he is Christ the
Lord. This will be a sign to you: You
will find a baby wrapped in cloths
and lying in a manger.*
*Luke 2:11, 12 NIV*

# CHRISTMAS JOY

Dear Jesus, Thank You
for Christmas!

Christmas is Your
birthday, Jesus.

The.

Christmas is angels, kings, and shepherds.

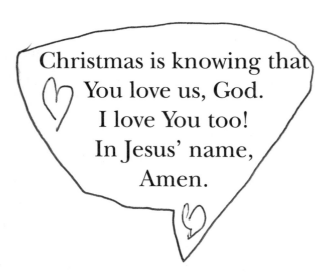

Christmas is knowing that
You love us, God.
I love You too!
In Jesus' name,
Amen.

## Parents—

Are you looking for fun ways to bring the Bible to life in the lives of your children?

Chariot Family Publishing has hundreds of books, toys, games, and videos that help you teach your children the Bible and apply it to their everyday lives. Look for these educational, inspirational, and fun products at your local Christian bookstore.

## CHARIOT
### FAMILY
### PUBLISHING
A DIVISION OF COOK COMMUNICATIONS

Credits:
*Thank You, Jesus\*; Friends; Babies Are for Loving; All Year Long; Home Is Best; Christmas Joy:* © 1985, 1986, 1987, 1988 Debby Anderson for text and illustrations.

*Three Cheers for Today; Today Is for Trusting; Hurray for Birthdays; Love Is Kind:*© 1985, 1986, 1987 L.B. Norton for text and Janet Warren Herbert for illustrations.

*Moms Are Special; Easter Is Here!:* © 1988 L.B. Norton for text and Bartholomew for illustrations.

All originally published as individual books in the *Sparklers* series.
\*Originally published as *Thank You, God.*